#ROOFTOP REVELATIONS

A 94-Day Faith Journey To Save A Community

Corey B. Brooks

Sermon To Book
www.sermontobook.com

#Rooftop Revelations / Corey B. Brooks
ISBN-13: 9780692372371
ISBN-10: 0692372377

I'd like to dedicate this book to every young black person whose life was gunned down by the brutality of violence that has now become an epidemic and every family of each victim still grieving the loss of their children. I'd also like to dedicate this book to every individual still fighting to eradicate violence, one neighborhood at a time.

I want to thank New Beginnings Church of Chicago for your unwavering support of the vision to save our community. You are the greatest church in the world! I also want to thank every supporter who helped us purchase the motel that has now been demolished and is making way for a new community and economic development center.

Lastly, I want to thank my wife and children, who paid the ultimate sacrifice of our family being apart for 94 days in an effort to save the lives of somebody else. I love you guys!

CONTENTS

HOODology 101

When I am with those who are weak, I share their weakness, for I want to bring the weak to Christ. Yes, I try to find common ground with everyone, doing everything I can to save some. — *1 Corinthians 9:22 (NLT)*

People need to know that you care, before they listen to what you have to share. — *Anonymous*

HOODology Defined

If you're anything like me, you have learned that there are some things in life that parents can't teach, schools can't educate, friends can't show you and a career can't pay you to do. There are some things in life that you won't know anything about until you have discovered them. I discovered HOODology!

When a child plays in the sand on a beach or in the backyard digging up dirt or in an alley between buildings, unintentionally, they will discover hidden treasures that may on the surface appear to be nothing more than worthless, expendable items. Items that were neglected, with no hope for a future, left to rot in the elements, watching life go by one second at a time. Does this sound familiar yet?

If you're reading this book, you're either from the hood, in the hood or curious about the hood.

I pastor a church in the hood on Chicago's south side called New Beginnings Church of Chicago, with people from the hood who act hood, talk hood, walk hood, dress hood, think hood and, ironically, love the hood! If you're reading this book, you're either from the hood, in the hood or curious about the hood.

Well, for those who are curious about the hood, let me offer you a definition that describes something that can only be understood, NOT by words, but by experience.

Hood: Derived from the word neighborhood, a term most recognized as an urban community; slang for ghetto, projects, usually a rundown area where poor, impoverished, uneducated, underprivileged people live.

Coupled with the suffix "ology", which is Latin for "the study of", we have HOODology.

HOODology? The urban dictionary defines HOODology as the social science of the inner city urbanite, transcending race, color or ethnicity. In short, the study of the hood!

HOODology is a modern day phenomena; it is a culture, a mindset, a method of salvation, a means to an end; it is misunderstood by many, but feared by most.

HOODology is a modern day phenomena; it is a culture, a mindset, a method of salvation, a means to an end; it is misunderstood by many, but feared by most. HOODology doesn't have a box or borders. It is creative by nature, bringing together the unconventional and the conventional. It is the weaving and cleaving of two entities, theology and hood life, uniquely separated but infinitely woven together.

I was practicing HOODology before I discovered what HOODology was. It took me getting involved in the lives of the members of my church outside of the Sunday and midweek settings to realize that people in the hood needed to know that I cared before they would listen to what I had to share. This came natural to me; I was very comfortable around people from the hood and the hood setting. Did I forget to mention that I live in the hood with my wife and children, just five minutes away from the church?

Using day-to-day hood experiences and relating them to a higher standard of living allows HOODology to create a method of discipleship. It requires a blend of biblical wisdom, knowledge and understanding played out in practical living to produce the desired results: a Changed Behavior!

I was amazed when I discovered that God teaches HOODology in the Bible: 1 Corinthians 9:22 says, "When I am with those who are weak, I share their weakness, for I want to bring the weak to Christ. Yes, I try to find common ground with everyone, doing everything I can to save some." (NLT)

HOODology is a life coach that speaks in a hood dialect so hood people can understand God, the Bible and themselves, NOT abandoning their love for the hood, but allowing God to be a part of it! This is not conventional; this is not what they teach you in seminary, but I was amazed when I discovered that God teaches HOODology in the Bible:

1 Corinthians 9:22 says, "When I am with those who are weak, I share their weakness, for I want to bring the weak to Christ. Yes, I try to find common ground with everyone, doing everything I can to save some." (NLT)

HOODology will challenge your theology! It has the propensity to cause you to examine yourself and those around you and to ask the proverbial question: "Am I doing enough to help my fellow man? Or, am I too self-centered to recognize that there's not a problem with the hood, there's a problem with me?"

CHAPTER ONE

The Theology Of HOODology

Understanding HOODology will teach you how to apply your creative and systematic approach at ministering to people in the hood. Failure introduced me to HOODology. Frustration caused me to get acquainted with HOODology. Faith taught me how to work HOODology. It wasn't until I suffered many failures and countless nights of frustration trying to figure out how to help so many people with so little resources, that I began to realize the theology of HOODology. I discovered what made HOODOlogy tick! I discovered the hard way, that what worked over there wouldn't necessarily work over here.

My church, perhaps like yours, had a BIG front door, but an even BIGGER back door, or several cracks in our foundation.

After 11 years of trial and error (with more errors than trials), HOODology started making sense. Being a pastor, it was natural to try to get people to understand the importance of prayer and a relationship with God through his son Jesus Christ. Like most churches, we would celebrate the new believers and their new life with Christ and celebrate their new opportunity for change. On the surface, this appeared to be enough, but it wasn't!

Herein lies the problem. Between the benediction and the next service is the HOOD! Sometimes, they never make it back, not because they don't want to, but because the Hood doesn't allow them to come back.

My church, perhaps like yours, had a BIG front door, but an even BIGGER back door, or several cracks in our foundation. The Spirit of the Lord would move on a service, the praise team would be in rare form, the people were ecstatic; the invitation to Christ would go forth and over seventy people would respond to the call. What could possibly be wrong with this? Benediction! They eventually had to leave the building and go home.

Once the service was over, after a couple of hours of the best feeling they ever had, how do you harness the emotional high? They were being hugged on by people they never knew, loved on like they'd never been loved on before, and for a brief moment in time, they cried tears of joy instead of tears of pain, if only it would have never ended.

For 70% of the people in my church, New Beginnings is their first church. On one hand this is good—they can be taught the proper way to relate to God, themselves and others—but on the other hand you can't expect them to help move the vision along, because they simply don't know. HOODology, when properly applied, fills the gap between services, so that those people God assigned to you will stay connected.

The New Members coordinator gathers their contact information and proceeds to give them the worst news they never saw coming. "Our next service is not until Thursday, mid-week Bible study (four days away). And if you miss it, we will see you next Sunday (seven days away)."

Herein lies the problem. Between the Benediction and the next service is the HOOD! Sometimes, they never make it back, not because they don't want to, but because the Hood doesn't allow them to come back.

For 70% of the people in my church, New Beginnings is their first church. On one hand this is good—they can be taught the proper way to relate to God, themselves and others—but on the other hand you can't expect them to help move the vision along, because they simply don't know. HOODology, when properly applied, fills the gap between services, so that those people God assigned to you will stay connected.

In the hood, there was no theology, only survival! I needed something else. You might be thinking, "Isn't God enough?" Yes he is, but he works through us! 1 Corinthians 9:22b says, "Yes, I try to find common ground with everyone, doing everything I can to save some." (NLT)

I realized my Dallas Theological and Grace Theological seminary education that taught me the Greek and Hebrew language, homiletics, hermeneutics, expository sermon prep, history of the Bible, apologetics and all that accompanied it, worked well in the confines of the four walls of the church. But in the hood, there was no theology, only survival! I needed something else. You might be thinking, "Isn't God enough?" Yes he is, but he works through us!

1 Corinthians 9:22b says, "Yes, I try to find common ground with everyone, doing everything I can to save some." (NLT)

HOODology bridges the gap between the Hood and Theology by teaching you how to introduce God to an urban environment and not only coexist, but lead others out by speaking their language without compromising God's commandments.

HOODology bridges the gap between the Hood and Theology by teaching you how to introduce God to an urban environment and not only coexist, but lead others out by speaking their language without compromising God's commandments. HOODology creates a platform for God to be presented, until he can be preached, through serving people not accustomed to being cared for.

HOODology showcases your creative expression of God in a way that causes the hood to recognize you with the highest honor, articulated with terms like, "You're really down to earth. I can respect what you're doing. You're not like most preachers; you don't mind talking to us, eating with us and living with us."

The theology of HOODology maintains a foundation built on three core values:

1) HOODology takes you where no man has ever gone before, or is just too afraid to go: the hood.

2) HOODology leverages the hood mentality by synergizing philosophies without compromise. You listen to the person, assess the need, listen some more, and when you're finished, you keep listening, even when the conversation is over. People in the hood have a deep desire to be heard. HOODology is all about listening in order to gain their respect and serving in order to gain their trust.

3) HOODology is a lifestyle that walks by faith and not by sight, looking beyond faults to the needs of the people, who need God and you! When I discovered HOODology, I discovered a passion within me that daily sought to help my fellow man. This was the day I became a Hoodologist!

CHAPTER TWO

Becoming A HOODologist

What is a Hoodologist? Before I give you the urban dictionary definition, understand this, being a Hoodologist is a calling. It's not for everybody; but for those who are called, the odds are you're probably operating as a Hoodologist and don't even know it. All you know is that you don't see things the way others do. You see value in the uneducated, deprived and underprivileged. What others avoid, you gravitate to. Strange? Not anymore. It's a Calling!

Hoodologist: Someone who understands urban culture, good and bad; a person who has gained, through experience, the expert knowledge on the art of their urban setting. A Hoodolo-

gist is a person who openly and objectively studies hood actions.

Hoodologist: Someone who understands urban culture, good and bad; a person who has gained, through experience, the expert knowledge on the art of their urban setting. A Hoodologist is a person who openly and objectively studies hood actions. The Hoodologist has his community under a microscope and is well-informed on the different levels of urbanite actions, communications and social classes in that same community.

God has a way of teaching you things, even when you're not trying to learn.

God has a way of teaching you things, even when you're not trying to learn. I can honestly say, I know I've been called to pastor New Beginnings Church of Chicago! The persecution I went through that caused me to start New Beginnings was all by design. I had to pastor a traditional church on the south side of Chicago at that exact time in my life, so I would know how to pastor a non-traditional church. I had to be persecuted, lied on, threatened, taken to court and even attacked. I had to lose a couple of battles in order to win the war.

Don't get me wrong; you don't know this while you're in this! All you know is, "I'm under attack and I don't like it." *Fight* or *Flight*. I decided to fight with the faithful few that stood with me; I decided I was not going to run from what I felt called to. Even though I had no clue what I was doing, I did know what I wasn't supposed to do—run. Just like the disciples of the Bible, persecution drove them out into other parts of the world, causing the greatest evangelistic movement known to man. As a result, the gospel of the Lord Jesus Christ was spread abroad, fulfilling the calling on their lives to *go*!

At the age of 19, there is absolutely no way you could have convinced me I was called to preach, not with the life I was living. It just didn't seem right; it wasn't fair to the people around me; it wasn't fair to me (I didn't deserve this assignment), and it wasn't fair to God.

There have been times when I've questioned my calling in life. At the age of 19, there is absolutely no way you could have convinced me I was called to preach, not with the life I was living. It just didn't seem right; it wasn't fair to the people around me; it wasn't fair to me (I didn't deserve this assignment), and it wasn't fair to God.

Maybe, just maybe, God slipped up on this one and mixed up the assignments. I felt as though I was the wrong Corey. I don't mind admitting that I have doubted myself and at times I've even doubted God. I know exactly how Moses felt when God told him he was going to lead his people out of bondage—instant Fear!

I've had my struggles with fear. Fear would cause me to second-guess myself as a man, a husband, a father, and as a pastor. Ultimately, the end result was costly. I'm sure something died as a result of my hesitation, (a ministry, a relationship, an idea, etc.) Consequently, I've learned through God's word to never wait for perfect conditions.

Ecclesiastes 11:4-6 says, "If you wait for perfect conditions, you will never get anything done. God's ways are as hard to discern as the pathways of the wind, and as mysterious as a tiny baby being formed in a mother's womb. Be sure to stay busy and plant a variety of crops, for you never know which will grow -- perhaps they all will." (NLT)

CHAPTER THREE

The Faith Journey

In November 2011, I was preparing to do the funeral of Carlton Archer, a 15-year-old young man who had been shot to death. It was my 10th teenage funeral that year. I had to convince his parents, who were members, to have the funeral at our church, all because they were afraid that the neighborhood gangs, seeing the young people from different neighborhoods, would show up and start trouble. Funerals in the hood are always an opportunity for the gangs to retaliate against a rival gang member. My thinking: not at this church!

In broad daylight, while young people were entering the church, that all- too- familiar noise rang out—bang, bang, bang!

I promised them that nothing would go wrong. I was wrong. Something happened that day that changed my life forever. In broad daylight, while young people were entering the church, that all- too- familiar noise rang out—*bang, bang, bang!*

During the funeral, I sensed a strong prompting of the Holy Spirit and I made an appeal for those who had guns on them, to turn them in and stop the killing! Four young men relinquished their semi-automatic weapons right there at the altar.

Down the street, gang members began shooting at the young people as they were entering the church. Needless to say, panic and chaos broke out. With over 1000 people in the sanctuary, I was in utter disbelief at what was happening. The war was on my front porch. An ancient enemy called violence was now invading what was perceived as a safe zone, the church.

Quickly, the police responded and restored order; it was only by the grace and mercy of God that no one was hurt. I preached the funeral, saddened because I was not able to keep my promise to those grieving parents and angry that the enemy called violence would so blatantly disrespect the house of God.

During the funeral, I sensed a strong prompting of the Holy Spirit and I made an appeal to those who had guns on them, to turn them in and stop the killing! Four young men relinquished their semi-automatic weapons right there at the altar. The emotions on that day were unbelievable and bittersweet. For the next several days, I could not rest, reflecting on the events that had transpired.

You must understand something about this motel. It was an eyesore for the community, dilapidated and a haven for illicit activity like prostitution, drug selling and drug usage. You name it, this abandoned motel was still open for business.

Desperate for change, I sought the Lord in prayer. On that same day, while looking out the window of my office, adjacent from an abandoned motel, I was still angry and complaining to God about what happened. You must understand something about this motel. It was an eyesore for the community, dilapidated and a haven for illicit activity like prostitution, drug selling and drug usage. You name it; this abandoned motel was still open for business. It was this day that I clearly heard the Lord speak to me regarding a faith journey that would define my purpose in life. This passage of Scripture continued to resonate in my spirit:

> *Why isn't the city of Chicago furious about the murder rate of these young people? Do they know what's happening or are they not aware? I can't be the only one feeling like this!*

Habakkuk 2:1-4 says, "I will climb up into my watchtower now and wait to see what the LORD will say to me and how he will answer my complaint. Then the LORD said to me, 'Write my answer in large, clear letters on a tablet, so that a runner can read it and tell everyone else. But these things I plan won't happen right away. Slowly, steadily, surely, the time approaches when the vision will be fulfilled. If it seems slow, wait patiently, for it will surely take place. It will not be delayed.'" (NLT)

I knew something had to be done! Others needed to know what was going on. This problem was running too rampant to be ignored. Why isn't the city of Chicago furious about the murder rate of these young people? Do they know what's happening or are they not aware? I can't be the only one feeling like this! Something had to be done, people needed to be aware of what was going on.

I am a product of community centers. Growing up, I strongly believe, if there hadn't been a community center to keep me occupied and active, I would have become another statistic in the morgue.

The Woodlawn Englewood communities needed a battle-tested solution that had a track record to support it—a community and economic development center. We needed a place where people could be taught how to improve their way of living and children would have a safe place to learn and play without the fear of stray or intentional bullets killing them. I am a product of community centers. Growing up, I strongly believe, if there hadn't been a community center to keep me occupied and active, I would have become another statistic in the morgue. My mother would have grieved my death and the cycle would continue.

Now what? I decided to face the problem in what some have called an unusual, yet radical, way. I would camp out in a tent on the rooftop of this abandoned motel until we raised enough money to purchase it, demolish it and build that community center. Simple!

It was wintertime in Chicago, a city notorious for its harsh weather conditions with wind chill factors that cause temperatures to consistently drop below zero. In addition to snow and ice storms, a wind flies off of Lake

Michigan, invading the city like the flying predator it is known by—"The Hawk!"

I anticipated I would be finished in about a month, so I went on a water-only fast for 21 days, showing God how serious I was about this cause and to create some urgency.

Chicagoans know how damaging The Hawk can be. When it comes in contact with any exposed flesh, without mercy, it will cut through your skin like a pack of needles being inserted at fifty miles per hour. Yet, as if God was sending a sign of comfort, we experienced one of the mildest winters in Chicago's history. The media even ran stories suggesting this was happening because I was on the roof. A lot of people don't know this, but I began to ponder this thought.

I was living on the rooftop of this motel, utilizing social media (Facebook and Twitter) as a means to garner support, communicate to others what I was doing and, more importantly, the purpose of why I was doing it. I anticipated I would be finished in about a month, so I went on a water- only fast for 21 days, showing God how serious I was about this cause and to create some urgency. Well, 90 plus days later, the fast was over, I was still on the roof, the story had made national and international news and I'd been given the name The Rooftop Pastor.

Our community was still under fire and young black males were still being gunned down. The community kept calling me and I kept calling the community. Whenever I would hear of a shooting, I would send a response team to report back the details. When phone calls started coming in from all over the community, seeking my advice and the help of our church, I became obsessed with fixing this problem of gun violence. My life, my family, and my church have all been turned upside down.

Something changed in me. I can't pinpoint the exact moment, but I knew something was different when another crying mother sought me out on the roof. She was trying to make sense out of the senseless death of her 15-year-old son being gunned down while standing in line to purchase some chicken, caught in the crossfire of a gun battle that had nothing to do with him.

I knew something was different when hurting fathers would cry on my shoulder, declaring, "I wish it was me!" I knew when teenage gang leaders, not even old enough to drive, would sit in that tent and seek guidance. The stories go on and on, but a lot of things were put into perspective regarding my specific calling and the ministry of our church.

In the end, I realized I had become a Hoodologist. This is true for anyone who becomes deeply connected to their community and their community becomes intimately connected to them. Nothing goes on without you being aware of it. And the funny thing is, when the community hurts, you hurt, and it hurts God.

CHAPTER FOUR

#Rooftop Revelations

In the solitude of the tent, I asked God, "How do you help people that appear so helpless, that appear to have no hope and no one to care about them? Why aren't people of influence running to the rescue? Do the lives of these children, who didn't ask to be here, matter?"

As The Lord spoke, I began to share these thoughts on social media. For me, this was very therapeutic, eye-opening, and inspiring, while for others, it was enlightening and encouraging.

True to His nature, God began to speak; he began to open up my understanding to what it means to sacrifice everything for the benefit of someone else. He began to give me #RooftopRevelations.

While living on that roof, I met so many people in and around the community, people of all backgrounds, nationalities and faiths and I realized that this endeavor to save a community had officially become a movement!

As The Lord spoke, I began to share these thoughts on social media. For me, this was very therapeutic, eye-opening, and inspiring, while for others, it was enlightening and encouraging.

While living on that roof, I met so many people in and around the community, people of all backgrounds, nationalities and faiths and I realized that this endeavor to save a community had officially become a movement! The movement was called ProjectH.O.O.D (Helping Others Obtain Destiny!).

What made it a movement? Collaboration! There was recognition by all people across the country that something had to be done about the gun violence plaguing our community and they were willing to get involved at whatever level they could in order to support the cause.

My team and I began to develop the ProjectH.O.O.D vision to end violence and build communities, one neighborhood at a time. Our mission was to empower people with the guidance, information and tools necessary to become peacemakers, problem solvers, leaders, and entrepreneurs in their communities. No one knew how ProjectH.O.O.D would become instrumental in the very near future for our community.

Amazingly, the most moving act within this movement happened when I received a $50.00 donation for the community center from a young African-American inmate incarcerated for murder. In his letter, he wrote, "Maybe if I would have had a community center to go to, I probably wouldn't be in jail today. Thank you for trying to help!" I literally cried after reading this and found much encouragement to forge ahead.

At this time, there were more murders and violence occurring in Chicago than the war in Iraq. All across urban America, Chicago was being called ChiRaq!

Like the aftermath of a natural disaster, this was a collaborative humanitarian effort to rescue our children who had become prisoners of war and violence was the oppressor. At that time, there were more murders and violence occurring in Chicago than the war in Iraq. All across urban America, Chicago was being called Chi-Raq!

During this rooftop experience, as I continued to pray and seek God for a deeper understanding, I began to tweet about it on Twitter. Thanks to the help of photographer Jason Thomas, you can take a walk with me through a photo journalistic faith journey of one man's attempt to save a community. #RooftopRevelations.

Project H.O.O.D.

Project H.O.O.D. (Helping Others Obtain Destiny) was a campaign to raise $450,000 to purchase land located at 6625 South King Drive in the Woodlawn neighborhood of Chicago for a community center on Chicago's Southside. The community center is to feature mixed- income housing, commercial spaces for businesses (small and large) to spark job creation, and areas for social services including expansion of New Beginnings Church's "Master's Academy." But the main goal is to provide children and families on the Southside of Chicago with the same resources and activities available in the more affluent neighborhoods.

Recognizing that the crime and violence, which are at epidemic proportions in the Woodlawn and Englewood areas, are symptoms of a greater problem, Pastor Brooks set out on a mission. He brought awareness through a rooftop vigil in a tent in Chicago in the dead of winter. The land is presently occupied by an abandoned motel whose rooftop Pastor Corey Brooks camped on for 94 days.

CHAPTER FIVE

The Pictorial Journey Through My Tweets

"We have to change the visual setting in the area, the mental landscape. This is why we need this community and economic center."
#RoofTopRevelations Feb. 13, 2012

"Somebody out there is asleep. God has called you to wake them up! You may never be Moses but you can be Jethro. Wake them up!" #RoofTopRevelations Feb. 15, 2012

"God will send people who are able to see what you see and usually they are people you've never even met." #RoofTopRevelations Feb. 15, 2012

"You can't get mad at people because they can't see what you see. Some people don't have the capacity to see it!" #Roof-TopRevelations Feb. 15, 2012

"I often wonder how many lives could have been saved if I had not been so blind to the needs around me. That hurts!" #RoofTopRevelations Feb. 15, 2012

*"There has not been a day that has gone
by that I have not asked God to forgive
me for not paying attention sooner."*
#RoofTopRevelations Feb. 15, 2012

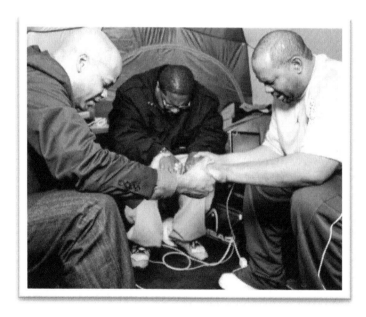

"The one you help save today may be the one who saves you tomorrow. We reap what we sow." #RoofTopRevelations Feb. 15, 2012

"Picture a day when all can walk to the park or take a stroll down the street for some ice cream and not feel terrified." #RoofTopRevelations Feb. 13, 2012

"*My heart now beats to the rhythm of sacrifice, courage, faith, love and peace.*"
#RoofTopRevelations Feb. 19, 2012

"My hands are on the pulse of Urban America and I know what I must do." *#RoofTopRevelations Feb. 19, 2012*

"My voice has become more profound as I declare from the rooftop, 'These killings must stop!'" #RoofTopRevelations Feb. 19, 2012

"In order to make a dream come true, it takes a lot of compassionate people working together." #RoofTopRevelations
Feb. 19, 2012

"I have become more aware of the need for collaboration. This is bigger than 1 man. This requires all of us!" #RoofTopRevelations Feb. 19, 2012

"My eyes have become more focused and now I can clearly see the problems and solutions." #RoofTopRevelations Feb. 19, 2012

"My mind has been stretched as I ponder the needs for Urban America." #RoofTopRevelations Feb. 19, 2012

"In 4 hours I would have been on the roof for 3 months. I was asked 'How do you feel about your decision to go on the roof?'" #RoofTopRevelations Feb. 19, 2012

"The best way I can explain it is to look at a caterpillar in a cocoon. He crawls in but he flys out!" #RoofTopRevelations
Feb. 19, 2012

"3 months ago, I crawled in not knowing what to expect, not knowing what God was up to. Little did I know this tent was my cocoon!" #RoofTopRevelations Feb. 19, 2012

"Don't let your haters talk you out of what you've been committed to!" #RoofTopRevelations Feb. 21, 2012

"When fear knocks at the door of commitment, don't answer!"
#RoofTopRevelations Feb. 21, 2012

"Count up the cost. Don't write a commitment that you know you can't cash!"
#RoofTopRevelations Feb. 21, 2012

"Make sure your actions out talk your mouth." #RoofTopRevelations Feb. 21, 2012

"If Jesus could hang in there for you, you ought to be able to hang in there for Him!" #RoofTopRevelations Feb. 21, 2012

"When your resources dry up, don't let your commitment dry up!" #RoofTopRevelations Feb. 21, 2012

"My feet are now ready to walk thru the valley of the shadow of death and I will fear no evil..." #RoofTopRevelations Feb. 21, 2012

"Somebody's life depends upon your commitment!" #RoofTopRevelations Feb. 21, 2012

"Commitment is easier when you're able to see that what you're committed to is greater than you!" #RoofTopRevelations Feb. 21, 2012

"Commitment is a marathon. When others fall off, you keep runnin'!"
#RoofTopRevelations Feb. 21, 2012

Proverbs 19:21 (MSG) We humans keep brainstorming options and plans, but God's purpose prevails. #RoofTopRevelations Feb. 22, 2012

Proverbs 19:6-7 (MSG) Lots of people flock around a generous person; everyone's a friend to the philanthropist. #RoofTopRevelations Feb. 22, 2012

Proverbs 19:4-5 (MSG) Wealth attracts friends as honey draws flies, but poor people are avoided like a plague. #Roof-TopRevelations Feb. 22, 2012

Proverbs 19:1-2 (MSG) Better to be poor and honest than a rich person no one can trust. #RoofTopRevelations Feb. 22, 2012

Proverbs 19:29 (MSG) The irreverent have to learn reverence the hard way; only a slap in the face brings fools to attention. #RoofTopRevelations Feb. 22, 2012

"If I allow you to to label me, it limits me. If you define me, it will confine me. Keep your labels!" #RoofTopRevelations Feb. 23, 2012

"You don't have to compete with every-body; you have enough competition against yourself." #RoofTopRevelations Feb. 23, 2012

"Copying makes you a copycat and you'll be second, at best!" #RoofTopRevelations Feb. 23, 2012

"Stop comparing yourself to others. You'll get frustrated trying to be like them or you'll become arrogant because you're better off than them." #RoofTo-pRevelations Feb. 23, 2012

"If you don't know who you are, people will make you what they want you to be!"
#RoofTopRevelations Feb. 23, 2012

"I am somebody; I don't have to drive what you drive, live where you live or wear what you wear. I am somebody!" #RoofTopRevelations Feb. 23, 2012

"Watch your focus. The greater things in life are usually not about things." #RoofTopRevelations Feb. 23, 2012

"Stop trying to impress others—especially people you don't even know and who may not even care." #RoofTopRevelations Feb. 23, 2012

"Some say that imitation is the greatest form of flattery. I don't think so, unless you're imitating the greatest: God!" #RoofTopRevelations Feb. 23, 2012

"You may as well just be you; everybody else is taken. That's when you're at your best!" #RoofTopRevelations Feb. 23, 2012

"What God starts, He finishes!" #Roof-TopRevelations Feb. 24, 2012

CHAPTER SIX

Conclusion: Day 94

February 24, 2012—It's the morning of Day 94 and my phone is ringing continuously from several callers. I answer one of the calls and the caller frantically states that Tyler Perry is going to give me the balance of the money to purchase the motel and they want me to call the radio station. After 94 days on this roof, I'm skeptical, but follow through anyway.

I connect to Syndicated Radio Show Host Tom Joyner, who states: "Pastor, you can come down off of the roof, Tyler Perry is going to donate the balance of the money needed to purchase the motel." Of course, I think it's a joke being played on me by one of my preacher friends, a prank call from Tom Joyner.

Turns out it wasn't a joke! Tyler heard about me being on the roof because a member of our church entered a contest inspired by Perry's movie, "Good Deeds," which had just been released. She wrote a 1 page letter sharing my rooftop story to help our community build a new center. Needless to say, I won!

Tyler Perry himself called me and I could hardly contain myself. Not only did Tyler donate the $98,000 balance toward the initial phase of the project, but I won the Harley Davidson motorcycle featured in the movie. Unbelievable! An hour later, ProjectH.O.O.D. received another donation of $85,000 from an anonymous Christian businessman who knew nothing about the Tyler Perry donation. I told him about it and he said he still wanted to make the first donation toward phase 2—the Community Center! I can't begin to say how overwhelmed I was. A press release went out announcing that I was coming down from the roof at 6 p.m. The media coverage and supporters that gathered that day were amazing.

The ProjectH.O.O.D. journey continues. At the time of this writing, we are still working to raise the funds to build the new center which will exceed $20 million dollars. ProjectH.O.O.D. has established a major footprint in the community and has since hosted several community events, partnered with the local police and is working with other community organizations to reduce violence, and increase employment and education conditions.

I will always be grateful to God for the 94-day rooftop assignment and every supporter who helped make a difference.

We still need help! Please pray for us and go to our website www.projecthood.org to help us gang up on the problem and not each other!

About The Author

As pastor, visionary, mentor, businessman, and philanthropist, Pastor Corey B. Brooks Sr., in November of 2000,with 250 charter members, founded New Beginnings Church of Chicago. It is an urban, non-denominational inner- city church on Chicago's south side, which now supports over 2,500 members.

Pastor Brooks is known for leading impactful community efforts to address the educational, economic, social and spiritual ills that burden inner- city communities. He has made national and international news for his unconventional, yet effective, stance against the senseless killings of young people by gun violence.

Deemed the "Rooftop Pastor" for living on the roof of an abandoned, dilapidated motel for 94 days and walking across America from New York to Los Angeles in over 4 months, his selfless acts have brought a greater awareness to the issues of violence and raised funds to help build a new community and economic development center, hopefully in the near future.

Recognized for his achievements, Pastor Brooks was appointed as Co-Chairman of Governor Bruce Rauner's transition team and was honored with the following prestigious awards: Best Community Leader of the year award by the Steve Harvey Ford Hoodie Awards, Chicago Defender's Newsmaker of the Year, and Chicago Urban League's Top Innovator award. Pastor Brooks ministered for Bishop TD Jakes' Pastors and Leaders conference in addition to sharing his story on the world- renowned TBN. He is highly sought after to teach others how to maximize their purpose by becoming relevant in the 21st century!

Pursuing a vision to eradicate violence one block at a time by offering hope, Pastor Brooks meets the people right where they are. He lives by the creed, *"It's time for us to Stop ganging up on each other and Start ganging up on the Problem!"*

A graduate of Ball State University and Grace Theological Seminary, Pastor Brooks is married to Delilah Brooks and they are the proud parents of four children.

"Thank You JESUUUSSS!!!" #RoofTo-pRevelations Feb 24, 2012 6:00pm

About SermonToBook.Com

SermonToBook.com began with a simple belief: that sermons should be touching lives, *not* collecting dust. That's why we turn sermons into high-quality books that are accessible to people all over the globe.

Turning your sermon or sermon series into a book exposes more people to God's Word, better equips you for counseling, accelerates future sermon prep, adds credibility to your ministry, and even helps make ends meet during tight times.

John 21:25 tells us that the world itself couldn't contain the books that would be written about the work of Jesus Christ. Our mission is to try anyway. Because, in Heaven, there will no longer be a need for sermons or books. Our time is now.

If God so leads you, we'd love to work with you on your sermon or sermon series.

Visit www.sermontobook.com to learn more.

All Problems in your past, present and future have a Purpose to fulfill in your life! The problems you are dealing with are leaving you frustrated, depressed and feeling like God has abandoned you. You've been praying for relief and you've even tried to borrow relief, but nothing is working. You constantly question, "Why all of these problems, God?"

Your Problems Have Purpose is an engaging book, full of practical life-application principles including:

- Discovering who you are in Christ
- Growing in God's purpose for you
- Learning how to overcome the fact that brokenness hurts
- Submitting to God's will for your life and living successfully

Additionally you'll learn...

- Exactly how God uses your problems to develop your purpose
- Why God uses problems to protect you from yourself
- What your purpose cost God

Discover how important your problems are to God's purposeful plan for your life, and how the RIGHT perspective makes all the difference!

Purchase today on Amazon.com!

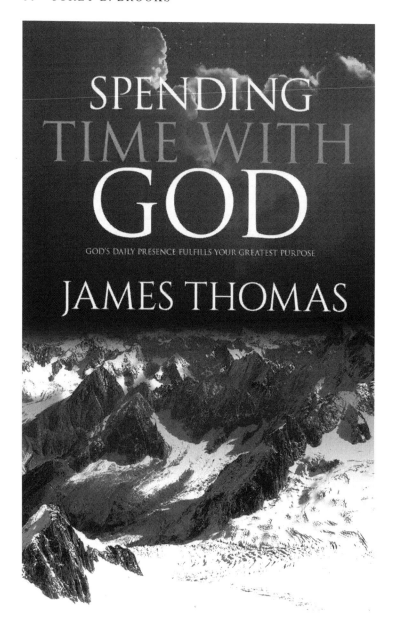

SPENDING
TIME WITH
GOD

GOD'S DAILY PRESENCE FULFILLS YOUR GREATEST PURPOSE

JAMES THOMAS

Spending time with God is one of the greatest privileges you have in life. Greater than your public worship, greater than your spiritual gifts, greater than preaching and teaching the gospel. When you commit yourself to spending time with your Heavenly Father on a daily basis, it will change your life. Period.

God wants to spend time with you, not because He's lonely, but because you so desperately need His daily presence in order to fulfill your greatest purpose.

In *Spending Time With God*, you'll learn super practical ways to draw near to your Heavenly Father and experience life-changing transformation as He draws near to you. For starters, you'll discover:

• 4 disciplines that motivate and inspire spending time with God

• The incredible impact of spending time with God

• Required elements for spending time with God

• The power of prayer and praise while spending time with God

Prepare yourself for the spectacular. Because when you experience God's daily presence, He fulfills your greatest purpose.

Purchase today on Amazon.com!

SCOTT SANDERS

HOLY
SPIRIT
TRAINING

DISCOVER THE PREDOMINANT
DIVINE POWER ON EARTH

If you've ever wondered if you've completely missed the purpose and ministry of the Holy Spirit, then this book might be a shocker for you.

There's a big difference between knowing the characteristics of the Spirit and knowing the Spirit as a person. The Holy Spirit is the predominant divine power on earth right now. But do you truly know Him?

In Holy Spirit Training, you'll train your senses to know there's more going on than what your eyes can see, discover how the Spirit is the key to accessing the "things" God has prepared for you, and learn exactly who the Spirit is and how He works. Get ready to discover:

• The role of the Holy Spirit in your life

• How to pick up the signals of the Holy Spirit

• How to follow and be led by the Holy Spirit

• How to partner with the Holy Spirit to manifest things on earth

Don't hesitate another day. Decide now to truly know the Holy Spirit and let Him guide you through life and put some *super* on your *natural*!

Purchase today on Amazon.com!

In the subtitle of this book, I chose the two themes of revelation and revolution because as I meditated on God loving me specifically and personally ... it transformed my Christianity.

Like stated in Romans 12:2, my mind was renewed and my Christian walk revolutionized. It dawned on me that my sins alone put Jesus on that cross. Had the world not consisted of billions of people and instead the world only consisted of little ole me, He still would have had to die. My personal sin debt was enormous. I was born in sin and shaped in iniquity. There were no two ways around it. Yet, He did what He did because He loved me. Always had, and always will. He loves me.

It is for this revelation alone that I wrote this book: so that you too can be revolutionized, like I was and still am being because it's a journey you never exit. Or ever want to. So I invite you to join me in a discovery of revelation and revolution as God unveils what it means to be loved by the Creator of the universe!

Purchase today on Amazon.com!